THE ROMANTASY KAMA SUTRA

Quarto.com

© 2025 Quarto Publishing

First Published in 2025 by Fair Winds Press, an imprint of The Quarto Group,
100 Cummings Center, Suite 265-D, Beverly, MA 01915, USA.
T (978) 282-9590 F (978) 283-2742

EEA Representation, WTS Tax d.o.o.,
Žanova ulica 3, 4000 Kranj, Slovenia.
www.wts-tax.si

Fair Winds Press titles are also available at discount for retail, wholesale, promotional,
and bulk purchase. For details, contact the Special Sales Manager by email at
specialsales@quarto.com or by mail at The Quarto Group, Attn: Special Sales Manager,
100 Cummings Center, Suite 265-D, Beverly, MA 01915, USA.

29 28 27 26 25   1 2 3 4 5

ISBN: 978-0-7603-9900-2

Digital edition published in 2025
eISBN: 978-0-7603-9901-9

Library of Congress Cataloging-in-Publication Data available.

Design and page layout: Justin Page
Cover image and illustrations: Giovanna Capel, @artsbygih

Printed in Hong Kong

The information in this book is for educational purposes only.
Any type of sexual activity should be consensual.

THE ROMANTASY KAMA SUTRA

64 Swoon-Worthy Sex Positions Inspired By Your Favorite Novels

QUIVER

CONTENTS

INTRODUCTION

Welcome to *The Romantasy Kama Sutra*. This Kama Sutra is for anyone who appreciates a low growl of (temporarily!) thwarted desire, an enemies-to-lovers arc, and a crushing hunger for each other that *must* find its satisfaction (probably in the last third of the book).

Here you'll find all kinds of the bendy sex positions that the Kama Sutra is known for, but with a romantasy spin. Like any great romantasy, these sex positions are part romance, part fantasy—all wrapped up in the steamy fire of lust, adventure, and white-hot passion. Some of these positions are intense and passionate (obvi), others are playful, rough, silly, or fun. Try some and see what you like. Figure out what stokes your flames higher—then do that.

There's lots of (very) old school Kama Sutra wisdom sprinkled throughout the book. You'll learn about different types of kisses, oral sex techniques, and foreplay to get you completely inflamed with longing. There's tips on stoking desire, like what to do when partners have different speeds of arousal or unequal levels of passion. And since ye olde Kama Sutra wasn't afraid of a little kink, you can also expect some tips on bondage, scratching, biting, and other roughhousing. Take whatever you need on your journey and leave the rest safely in these pages.

HOW TO USE THIS BOOK

I s romantasy about the romance or the fantasy? Yes. And truly amazing sex is part romance, part fantasy, too.

This book is for finding new ways to sweep each other off your feet. It's based on the Kama Sutra, but romantasy-ed up with fiery passion, slow burn romantic energy, and plenty of chances to do some sexual world building of your own.

The 64 positions here are gender-neutral and fully adjustable. They can work for whatever sexuality you've got going on—whether you're two heroes, two heroines, one of each, or have a faerie/human situation happening. To keep it adjustable for your needs, we're using the terms "giver" for the person penetrating and/or giving oral sex and "receiver" for the person receiving penetration or oral.

Many of the penetrative positions can work anally or vaginally, and if no one in your realm possesses a penis, go ahead and fill your bag of provisions with a strap-on, if you'd like. Or, hell, get two. There are plenty of portals to passion that can be filled.

There are lots of suggestions in this book, but go ahead and make your own tweaks by adding toys, hands, mouth—anything that will make it better for you. And if you want to don armor, dragon wings, or anything else, go right ahead. What happens in your bed chambers stays in your bed chambers.

Feeling the flutterings of anticipation? Let the quest begin.

WHAT YOU I WANT

SHOULD ALWAYS MATTER

—JENNIFER L. ARMENTROUT, *FROM BLOOD AND ASH*

THE SEAL OF THE FIRST KISS

THE EPIC FIRST TASTE OF EACH OTHER

THE ORACLE'S INSTRUCTIONS:

This is the kind of intense kiss that happens about a third of the way through a novel when lips finally—finally!—meet for the first time. To do it, just lean in close and touch your lips together.

THE RAVISHING:

This is gentle kiss to start exploring each other. Get close and breathe in each other's scent and notice how your mouths feel against each other. Pay attention to how your bodies react to each other—a kiss is a preview of what's to come.

UNLOCK THE SECRET WISDOM:

Breathe together while your lips just barely touch to bring yourselves into the moment. Take an extra beat or two before you actually touch your lips together to draw out the moment.

HARNESS THE FORBIDDEN POWER

If you'd like to follow the original text of Kama Sutra, add a "throbbing kiss" by pulsing the bottom lip when the lips touch. Or a "touching kiss" when you dart your tongue out like a serpent and touch your lover's lips. Or try the "upper lip," which is sucking the upper lip of your partner while your lower lip is sucked.

2

THE ASTRAL KISS
PLOT OBSTACLES BE DAMNED! THIS KISS IS HAPPENING!

THE ORACLE'S INSTRUCTIONS:

Slide into each other's arms and start kissing in earnest.

THE RAVISHING:

This kiss takes things further. Start by focusing on each other's lips and tongue.

UNLOCK THE SECRET WISDOM:

Take yourself on a journey over your partner's entire body. Stay awhile and linger on less obvious spots like the eyelids, earlobes, back of the knee, arch of the foot, belly, inner arm, and/or the nape of the neck. Before you kiss a spot, take a moment and just hover over it with your mouth and let your partner feel your warm breath.

HARNESS THE FORBIDDEN POWER

The Kama Sutra describes four styles of kissing and what body parts they're for. Try the "soft kiss," using gentle nips and licking on your partner's chest and various crevices. The "moderate kiss" is nibbling with teeth and used on the cheeks, breasts, hips, and belly. The "full-on kiss" is kissing the whole body and licking your partner's curves. If your partner is part beast, literally or metaphorically, try a "contracted kiss," which is adding a little scratching to your partner's lips and body.

THE ENCHANTED HOLLOW
THE MOST INTIMATE KISS

THE ORACLE'S INSTRUCTIONS:

The receiver lies on the edge of the bed with their legs spread. The giver kneels on the floor with their head between their partner's legs. The giver presses their mouth on their partner's vulva to stake their claim.

THE RAVISHING:

This is just a starter move to show your partner what they're in for. The giver doesn't take it too deep—they just press their lips to the vulva.

UNLOCK THE SECRET WISDOM:

The giver should take it real slow to let their partner warm up. They can start by pressing their open mouth next to that vulva and gently breathing nice warm breaths. Then they can add their hands to rub and love up their partner's belly, thighs, and boobs.

HARNESS THE FORBIDDEN POWER

In the Kama Sutra, women and their vulvas (aka yoni or lotus flower in the Kama Sutra) were given respect for being the source of life. The idea was that stimulating the vulva releases sexual energy which flows out in juices. If you drink these juices, you fill yourself with that sexual energy and power. Even if you don't necessarily believe that, if you act as though it's true, it will make for a glorious session of oral.

4

THE MAGE'S WHISPER

HOW TO SPEAK PUSSY

THE ORACLE'S INSTRUCTIONS:

The receiver stands with their legs apart. The giver kneels in front of them between their legs and spreads open their outer lips (that fleshy part of the vulvas). If the receiver doesn't want to stand, they can sit down or lie back onto a nice comfy bed.

THE RAVISHING:

The giver licks up the shaft of the clitoris, running their tongue up each side, then adding long, slow sucks.

UNLOCK THE SECRET WISDOM:

Try some Kama Sutra moves on your partner by starting with soft and shallow tongue flicks along the shaft of the clitoris, then move to gently sucking on the clitoris and rolling your tongue over it.

HARNESS THE FORBIDDEN POWER

Want to try for some squirting? Test out "the kiss of the penetrating tongue" where the giver thrusts their tongue inside of the vagina, then slides it back out, repeating and increasing speed as their partner gets closer to orgasm. For a more intense sensation, the giver can also focus their tongue on the clit and vulva and slide a finger or two inside, pressing on the upper wall of the vagina. Squirting might happen or it might not—either option is amazing (and normal)!

THE STROKING OF THE DRAGON'S TAIL
UNSHEATHING THAT SACRED SWORD

THE ORACLE'S INSTRUCTIONS:

The receiver can either sit on a chair, stand, or lie down in a bed with their hips right at the edge. The giver kneels between their partner's legs to take their steely rod into their mouth.

THE RAVISHING:

The giver takes their partner's penis halfway into their mouth, using lots of suction—like sucking on a particularly bewitching lollipop.

UNLOCK THE SECRET WISDOM:

Make it feel very personal by staying really connected with your partner while it's all happening. The giver can look up into the receiver's eyes while taking that penis in their mouth. The receiver can, and should, let their partner know what's working and what's not. Want more? Less? Harder? Softer? Feedback is good. If it feels awkward to say it outright, the receiver can stroke the giver's hair and guide their partner's head gently or let them know via moans how much they like what's happening.

HARNESS THE FORBIDDEN POWER

Try a Kama Sutra-style "side nibbling lingam kiss." The giver holds their partner's penis with their fingers and kisses and nibbles in a gentle manner up and down each side of the shaft.

THE SERPENT'S CARESS
CHARMING THE SERPENT

THE ORACLE'S INSTRUCTIONS:

Find a position that feels comfortable for both of you. You can try lying down, having the receiver standing and holding onto a wall with the giver kneeling, or the receiver sitting with the giver kneeling on the floor.

THE RAVISHING:

This is the Kama Sutra version of deep throating. The giver takes their partner into their mouth and slides it as far back into their throat as feels comfortable. If there's gagging, that's normal. Some people are turned on by it, some aren't. Figure out what's comfortable for both of you.

UNLOCK THE SECRET WISDOM:

To make deep throating easier, the giver can open the back of their throat by pretending to yawn. Breathe easily through your nose, taking the penis in slowly. And if the giver doesn't like deep throating, they can either stop and switch to a regular, good old-fashioned BJ *or* make it a fake-out deep throat by wrapping their lubed-up hand around the base of the penis to mimic the feel.

HARNESS THE FORBIDDEN POWER

For the fullest deep throating possible, the giver can lie on a bed with their head hanging back over the edge. The receiver stands at the side and the giver pulls them in as deep as they'd like by holding onto their butt cheeks.

THE BONDED PAIR

THE MOST FORBIDDEN KISS OF ALL

THE ORACLE'S INSTRUCTIONS:

Both of you lie on your bed, or lair, depending. Turn on your sides facing each other but flipped in opposite directions so your mouths are near each other's groins. Arrange yourselves so that you both can comfortably love up each other's penis or vulva with mutual oral sex. You can also try it with one person lying on top of the other—see what works.

THE RAVISHING:

Use your mouths to kiss, lick and suck your partner's throbbing loins.

UNLOCK THE SECRET WISDOM:

Try mirroring each other's moves to take the bonding further. If your partner quickens their pace, then you go faster as well. Are they taking it slow and sexy? Then slow it down to match their pace. If it's too hard to focus on pleasuring your partner and taking your own pleasure at the same time, go ahead and take turns being the ravisher then the ravished.

HARNESS THE FORBIDDEN POWER

If you want to use sex toys to enhance your pleasure, assemble an arsenal of things you might require on your journey. You can add butt plugs (vibrating or not), bullets, wand or clitoral suction vibes, prostate vibrators and/or penis sleeves.

THE MYSTIC SPIRAL
A MORE MYSTICAL VERSION OF 69

THE ORACLE'S INSTRUCTIONS:

One of you lies on the bed with their legs spread and their head hanging over the side. The other person stands by the partner's head and leans over to put their penis or vulva in their partner's mouth and puts their own mouth between their partner's legs.

UNLOCK THE SECRET WISDOM:

If the person standing is feeling nice and strong, they can lift their partner's hips and lick and nibble their partner's thighs and/or press their penis or vulva more firmly against their mouth.

THE RAVISHING:

Use your mouth and your hands to drive that partner of yours to ecstasy while they're doing the same to you.

HARNESS THE FORBIDDEN POWER

Use your hands to enhance the actions of your mouth. Hold onto each other's butt cheeks to squeeze or pull each other closer. Slide a finger inside a vagina to rub the upper wall. Circle a wet thumb and forefinger around the base of the penis shaft. Give love to a set of balls with gentle sucking, long licks, or just cupping them with a hand. Slide a lubey finger in each other's asses. Decide amongst yourselves. Your adventure, your rules.

THE CELESTIAL UNION

MISSIONARY ON A HIGHER PLANE

THE ORACLE'S INSTRUCTIONS:

The receiver lies on their back with their legs bent. The giver kneels by their partner's hips, puts one hand on either side of their head, and leans over their body. The receiver raises one leg and places it over their partner's shoulder, then straightens their other leg. The giver straightens the same leg on the same side (i.e., giver's left, receiver's right). The giver's tucked leg is the same one that the receiver has over their shoulder (i.e., giver's right, receiver's left).

THE RAVISHING:

You can thrust, grind, or bob up and down.

UNLOCK THE SECRET WISDOM:

Whether you decide to go in anally or vaginally, this position works for deep or shallow penetration. This is a bonus if you're working with an extra-large or extra-small penis or strap-on. For deeper penetration, the receiver pulls their raised knee back further; for more shallow penetration, the receiver pushes back with their leg against the giver's chest.

HARNESS THE FORBIDDEN POWER

Try switching legs during. It keeps anyone from getting sore, plus during the transition, the receiver can squeeze their vaginal or anal muscles around the penis or strap-on.

THE PULL OF THE CRESCENT MOON

GET EVEN MORE OF EACH OTHER

THE ORACLE'S INSTRUCTIONS:

The receiver lies on their back, tucking their knees up to their chest. If they want, they can hold their knees in place with their arms or hands for more support. The giver kneels by their partner's backside to penetrate.

THE RAVISHING:

The giver can penetrate either anally or vaginally and pump away. If they're going in too deep, the receiver can press their feet against their partner's chest to control the depth.

UNLOCK THE SECRET WISDOM:

Put a sex wedge or a firm pillow or two under the receiver's hips for comfiness and to get body parts exactly where you want them to go. The receiver can also rock their hips up and down to switch up the stimulation for both partners.

HARNESS THE FORBIDDEN POWER

The Kama Sutra lists several ways of thrusting, and this position works well with a swirling method. The giver holds their penis or strap-on in their hand and swirls it around inside their partner's bum or vagina. If the receiver has a vulva, the giver can also pull out throughout and swirl their head in a circle around their partner's clit.

11

THE SACRED COUPLING

LET YOUR BODIES AND SOULS COME TOGETHER

THE ORACLE'S INSTRUCTIONS:

The receiver lies flat on their back with their legs straight and slightly spread. The giver lies flat on top of their partner so that they're completely covering their body and then stretches their legs straight between their partner's legs. Both of you can stretch your arms over your head so you can hold hands.

THE RAVISHING:

Keep holding hands, look into each other's eyes, and use slow, deep thrusts. For a tighter feel with penetrative sex, the receiver can move their legs between their partner's and press them tightly together.

UNLOCK THE SECRET WISDOM:

If the person on the bottom has a vulva, the receiver can shift their body up slightly so their partner can get more clit stimulation by pressing against their pubic bone. If a penis or strap-on is involved, the person on top moves up enough so that the top of their penis/strap-on is rubbing over the clit. Instead of thrusting, use more of a rocking or grinding motion, letting the bottom person guide the speed, motion, and pressure.

HARNESS THE FORBIDDEN POWER

Throw down some old sheets or towels; cover yourselves in a bunch of lube, massage oil, or other magic elixirs and slide your bodies together.

12

THE STARLIT EMBRACE

PERFECT FOR WHEN YOU JUST WANT TO LIE DOWN AND BASK IN EACH OTHER'S RADIANCE

THE ORACLE'S INSTRUCTIONS:

One partner lies on their right side and the other one lies on their left side. You face each other, wrapping your legs and arms around each other to get as intimate as possible.

THE RAVISHING:

One or both partners can control the movement. Try moving gently against each other using your legs for leverage.

UNLOCK THE SECRET WISDOM:

Use the Starlit Embrace as a way to really focus on each other. If one of you tends to orgasm quickly, this is a great position for slowing down to give the person who takes longer a chance to catch up. The speedier one can also reach down and give the slower one a hand. Or take a moment to explore a side quest of oral sex.

HARNESS THE FORBIDDEN POWER

If a penis or strap-on is involved, you can get more stimulation going with a penis ring—a vibrating version will add even more rumbly sensations. If there are two vulvas involved, try a double-headed dildo that vibrates to give both of you an extra buzz.

THE PROTECTOR
DISCOVER THE SECRET TREASURE WITHIN

THE ORACLE'S INSTRUCTIONS:

The receiver lies on their back and brings their knees up to their chest. The giver squats by their partner's butt and leans over their partner's body, resting their weight on their hands. The giver puts their thighs outside of their partner's and presses together tightly.

THE RAVISHING:

The giver presses their thighs together to make for a tighter feel for both of you. The giver should also make sure to be angling their penis or strap-on so it's pointing upward for well-targeted stimulation of a G-spot or P-spot. Using a rocking motion can help.

UNLOCK THE SECRET WISDOM:

The receiver will have their hands free so they can stroke themselves or hold onto a small toy. If anyone gets sore, switch to something else for a while.

HARNESS THE FORBIDDEN POWER

For better support and movement, plus more directed internal stimulation for the receiver, the giver can hold up their partner by the hips or butt. Or go ahead and let a pillow or two do the work. Use a sex pillow, or you can DIY it with regular pillows or sofa cushions.

THE MERMAID'S WISH

PUT THOSE NEW LEGS TO GOOD USE

THE ORACLE'S INSTRUCTIONS:

The receiver lies on their back, crossing their legs and lifting them up to their stomach. The giver kneels by their partner's butt with their knees spread widely apart. The giver can either keep their legs tucked under them or bend them behind along the bed. The receiver wraps their legs around their partner's waist, crossing their ankles behind their partner's back. The giver keeps their back straight and bends slightly over their partner's body, holding them by their knees, or lying further over their body and resting their weight on their hands.

THE RAVISHING:

The giver can thrust away à la missionary style, but it also works with a slow grind if the receiver wants to use their legs to pull their partner in even deeper.

UNLOCK THE SECRET WISDOM:

The giver can extend the pleasure by mixing penetration with break-out sessions of oral sex.

HARNESS THE FORBIDDEN POWER

Make it extra romantic by starting with a long, slow massage. Light some candles and use a luxurious scented oil (keep oils out of vaginas). Extra magical points if you heat the oil in a bowl of warm water beforehand.

THE FINAL GAUNTLET

A CHALLENGE FOR ONLY THE BRAVEST OF WARRIORS

THE ORACLE'S INSTRUCTIONS:

The receiver lies on their back and curls their legs up as far over their head as they can. (Have care, now.) The giver squats above their partner, holding their thighs back to penetrate. Instead of using the receiver as a chair, the giver uses their thigh muscles and feet for balance. The giver holds the receiver's thighs open for support and to go in as deep as you both can handle.

THE RAVISHING:

The giver can plunge up and down like they're churning sweet cream or they can mix it up with some stirring motions.

UNLOCK THE SECRET WISDOM:

Keep it slow and steady, stooping to breathe and make sure everyone's doing okay. If things feel unsteady, the receiver can spread their arms out to the sides for balance.

HARNESS THE FORBIDDEN POWER

The receiver is basically doing the Plow position in yoga, so perfecting those skills makes this position easier. The receiver can practice by lying on their back and bringing their legs as far back as they can, trying to stretch a little more with each exhale. The goal is to be able to get their knees by their ears or even get their legs straight.

THE DANCE OF THE VICTORS

MAKE A V FOR VICTORY

THE ORACLE'S INSTRUCTIONS:

The receiver lies on their back with their legs straight up in the air in a V-shape. The giver kneels between the partner's legs and takes an ankle in each hand, spreading their thighs apart and holding their legs. For better leverage and more comfort, the giver can also stand next to the bed.

THE RAVISHING:

The giver can go in anally or vaginally. As you move, take advantage of the great view of each other.

UNLOCK THE SECRET WISDOM:

The giver can move the receiver's legs to change the angles. Try pressing their legs together, holding both to one side, or opening and shutting them like scissors.

HARNESS THE FORBIDDEN POWER

Indulge the ancient forbidden arts of voyeurism and/or exhibitionism. The receiver can put on a little show by pinching and squeezing their nipples or playing with themselves using a hand or toy while the giver gets the best viewing spot in the kingdom. If the giver wants to show off their glory, they can pull out and stroke themselves slowly until neither of you can take it anymore.

THE CASTLE DOORS

THROW OPEN THE CASTLE DOORS AND LET THE GAMES BEGIN

THE ORACLE'S INSTRUCTIONS:

The receiver lies on their back, placing their palms under their bum and arching their hips to the ceiling. They spread their thighs as wide as they can, keeping their feet as close to their hips as possible. From there, the giver has some choices: They can sit in front of their partner with their legs straight out or they kneel or crouch between their partner's legs. Once situated, the giver grabs a hold of their partner's thighs to enter.

THE RAVISHING:

The giver holds on and thrusts or grinds.

UNLOCK THE SECRET WISDOM:

The giver would get many blessings from the gods if they use a hand or two to stroke their partner's penis or vulva.

HARNESS THE FORBIDDEN POWER

If the receiver has a vulva, the Kama Sutra has some ideas for that. These tricks also work for anal sex. The receiver can:
1) Display the Kegel's/butt squeezing practice they've been doing by squeezing around their partner's penis or strap-on.
2) Keep their thighs spread as wide as possible. This is especially good if their partner's steely member is Pegasus-sized.
3) Press their thighs together tightly. This one is good if their partner's throbbing manhood (or strap-on hood) is smaller-sized.

THE STAR-CROSSED LOVERS

THIS QUEST REQUIRES GREAT TRAINING

THE ORACLE'S INSTRUCTIONS:

The receiver lies on their back with their legs crossed or, if they're very flexible, in the Lotus position: legs crossed and each foot on the opposite thigh. The giver kneels so they're penetrating while pressing their partner's thighs to open their legs wide. If the receiver is uncomfortable, they can draw their legs up as far as they'll go so that their calves touch their thighs and their knees touch their chest. Or they can just take the easy path and lift their legs however they damn well please.

THE RAVISHING:

This position tilts the receiver's pelvis to get more contact with their partner's pelvic bone, so if the receiver has a vulva, they get more clit stimulation. Take advantage of this alchemy by grinding and rubbing against each other.

UNLOCK THE SECRET WISDOM:

For deeper penetration, or if the receiver's legs are tired, they can unfold their legs and put them up onto their partner's chest.

HARNESS THE FORBIDDEN POWER

A couple's vibrator will help lift you both into another cosmos. Try something wearable like a cock ring or an insertable couple's toy for hands-free, buzzy love.

THE WINDSWEPT RAPTURE

WORLD BUILDING FOR TWO

THE ORACLE'S INSTRUCTIONS:

The receiver lies on their back with their legs crossed and feet on their thighs—or if that's not working, experiment with different leg positions until you get to something close to that. The giver leans over their partner's body, holding themselves on their hands and knees.

THE RAVISHING:

Make it extra romantic and activate the vibe of the "fated mates" trope by moving slowly and staring into each other's eye.

UNLOCK THE SECRET WISDOM:

Lean into the romance—love each other up by stroking each other's faces and bodies and whispering words of your love and long-denied passion.

HARNESS THE FORBIDDEN POWER

This is a good anal position, especially for beginners, because the receiver can control how deep the penis or strap-on goes. If it's too much, the receiver can slow it down or back it up a bit by pressing their feet and calves against their partner's belly. As with all anal, make sure the receiver is aroused and ready before doing any penetration. Go very slowly and let the receiver guide the speed. Use a ton of lube designed for anal because butts aren't self-lubricating.

THE MAGICK MENAGERIE

EMBRACE YOUR INNER BEAST

THE ORACLE'S INSTRUCTIONS:

The receiver rocks onto their back, holding their ankles in each hand as they raise their feet. The giver crouches monkey-like between their partner's legs. The giver can slap and kiss their partner's chest playfully before penetrating, but OPTIONAL with the slapping part.

THE RAVISHING:

The Kama Sutra is big on using animals as inspiration for positions. This one involves embracing your inner monkey—it's all about playfulness, laughing, and having fun. The idea is to embrace your monkeyness and have a good laugh together. Romantasy is generally down with non-human love interests, so you're good to go.

UNLOCK THE SECRET WISDOM:

Go ahead and shriek and squeal or make whatever primitive animal sounds you're feeling. Sex is weird and silly and awkward—just ride with it.

HARNESS THE FORBIDDEN POWER

Go full-on monkey by taking turns wielding a vibrator and acting like you don't know what it's for. Press it against each other's chest, hands, thighs, inner arms and see what happens. People with a vulva usually like vibrators on or near their clits or against their vulvas. People with a penis might like a vibrator pressed against the bottom of the shaft or their perineum (the area between the balls and the butt hole). See what works!

THE UNICORN'S HOOF

PUT YOUR BEST FOOT (OR HOOF) FORWARD

THE ORACLE'S INSTRUCTIONS:

The receiver lies on their back with one leg outstretched along the bed. They raise their other leg, putting their foot (or hoof, if they're half-beast) on their partner's forehead. The giver kneels between their partner's thighs, pressing against their thigh as they thrust.

THE RAVISHING:

Add a little something extra to the usual thrusting. The giver can rub their partner's penis or vulva with a hand or toy or squeeze their partner's thigh while the receiver rubs themselves. The receiver can give their partner's butt some affectionate squeezes.

UNLOCK THE SECRET WISDOM:

To switch up sensations, the giver can raise or lower the angle of penetration by scooting up or down and the receiver can switch it up and control the depth by pressing their foot more lightly or harder against their partner's forehead.

HARNESS THE FORBIDDEN POWER

Go harder on the foot aspect with some foot play. The giver can kiss the soles of their partner's feet, lick their way up the arch, or take each toe in their mouth and individually suck on them.

THE CHURNING OF THE TIDES

MAKE YOURSELVES DIZZY WITH LUST

THE ORACLE'S INSTRUCTIONS:

The giver lies flat on the bed, their legs slightly spread. The receiver squats over their partner and straddles them. The receiver keeps their knees up, with their feet flat on either side of their partner.
The receiver rides there a while, then rotates their entire body 90 degrees so they're riding sidesaddle while keeping their partner's penis or strap-on inside of them. If you both are into it, keep it going with the receiver doing another quarter turn so they're facing away from their partner's face. Complete the circuit with two more turns so that the receiver has faced all four directions of the compass. Repeat as much as you'd like.

THE RAVISHING:

The receiver can rock back and forth, squeeze, and/or ride their partner.

UNLOCK THE SECRET WISDOM:

The polite thing is to give the receiver free rein to do whatever makes them feel comfortable. They can lean back, lean forward, or just perch atop the giver for a bit and play with themselves.

HARNESS THE FORBIDDEN POWER

Try it with oral. The person on top straddles or kneels next to their partner so their mouth loves up that penis/vulva from four different directions.

MY ENTIRE WORLD CONSTRICTED TO THE TOUCH

OF HIS LIPS ON MY SKIN

-SARAH J. MAAS, *A COURT OF THORNS AND ROSES*

THE LADY KNIGHT
TAKE A VICTORY LAP WITH REVERSE COWGIRL

THE ORACLE'S INSTRUCTIONS:

The giver lies on their back, resting on their arms or using pillows behind their arms and back for support. The receiver straddles their partner's hips facing away from them and rests their hands on their partner's calves or thighs.

THE RAVISHING:

In the Kama Sutra's version of cowgirl, the receiver does a gentle rocking or swinging motion instead of the usual up or down thrusting. And the giver? They just lie back and enjoy the ride.

UNLOCK THE SECRET WISDOM:

If the receiver grows weary on their hero's journey, they can rise up on all fours so they're hovering instead of sitting on their partner. Once they're hovering aloft, the receiver can rub themselves with a hand or toy while the giver thrusts up into them.

HARNESS THE FORBIDDEN POWER

If the receiver wants to earn the highest honors in their realm, they can contract their Kegel muscles or their anus around their partner's penis, squeezing and holding in sync with their rocking. (If their partner has a strap-on, this move is less award-winning but will still enhance it for the receiver.)

THE MYSTICAL VORTEX

IF YOU HAVE ANY MAGIC SPELLS, NOW'S THE TIME TO USE THEM

THE ORACLE'S INSTRUCTIONS:

The receiver lies on their back with their legs stretched out in front of them and slightly spread. The giver lies on top of their partner, enters missionary style, and penetrates for as long as they'd like. Then, slowly and carefully, they turn themselves around—keeping their penis or strap-on inside of their partner—so that their head is between their partner's feet and their feet are on either side of their partner's head. Try that for a bit, then return, doing 180s as long as you both want and/or are able.

THE RAVISHING:

This is kinda tricky, so do whatever type of movement will keep you both riding comfortably. You might be moving differently at each stop. Do what works.

UNLOCK THE SECRET WISDOM:

If you have two vulvas onboard, a flexible double-headed dildo is great for handling the turns.

HARNESS THE FORBIDDEN POWER

If you like doing the switcheroo, add two extra stops. Instead of going head-to-head then foot-to-foot, try stopping in between so that you two are lying perpendicularly to each other. And like The Churning of the Tides (page 54), this can work better as an oral position.

THE TAMING OF THE HEADSTRONG APPRENTICE

PLAY WITH AN ENEMIES–TO–LOVERS STORY ARC

THE ORACLE'S INSTRUCTIONS:

The receiver lies on their back and the giver kneels in front. The receiver pulls their hips up so they're resting on their partner's thighs, then bends their knees, pulling their thighs to their chest. The receiver then presses the soles of their feet against their partner's chest.

THE RAVISHING:

Whether you're doing this anally or vaginally, the receiver has a lot of control. They can press their legs together for a tighter feel or they can change the depth and intensity by adjusting how hard they press their feet against their partner's chest.

UNLOCK THE SECRET WISDOM:

Both the receiver and the giver have their hands free to rub the receiver's penis or vulva with a hand or toy.

HARNESS THE FORBIDDEN POWER

Want to try some Dom/sub play? The giver can control the motion by holding their partner's hips and rocking them back and forth, using their partner's body like a sex toy or Fleshlight. The Dom can boss their sub around verbally by using commands like "Squeeze that sexy ass/pussy for me" or making the sub beg for more. (With all sex stuff, get enthusiastic consent before and during.)

THE MASKED BALL
A HORIZONTAL WALTZ

THE ORACLE'S INSTRUCTIONS:

The receiver lies on their back and the giver kneels by their hips. The giver raises their partner's hips onto their thighs and the receiver pulls their thighs to their chest until penetration. Then the receiver puts one foot on their partner's chest and stretches the other leg straight out over their partner's thighs.

THE RAVISHING:

As the giver thrusts, the receiver moves their straight leg up and down. The movement will make the receiver's anus or vagina tighten naturally, leading to a tighter, ever-changing fit.

UNLOCK THE SECRET WISDOM:

The receiver can mix up the sensations by changing which leg is the straight one.

HARNESS THE FORBIDDEN POWER

Throw down some old towels or blankets and douse yourselves in copious amounts of lube. Smear it on each other's chests, cover your thighs and bellies, and slather lube between each other's legs. Run your hands and bodies all over each other's slipperiness. Afterward, you can rinse off together in the shower or a nearby enchanted waterfall.

THE ETERNAL BOND

BASK IN YOUR FATED LOVE

THE ORACLE'S INSTRUCTIONS:

The receiver lies on their back, crossing their legs at the ankles. They pull their legs up and keep their thighs together and close to their chest so they can rest their feet on their partner's chest. The giver kneels at their partner's hips to enter and holds on tight.

THE RAVISHING:

This is great for deep penetration, either anally or vaginally, but if it's too deep, the receiver can use their feet to guide how deep they want to take a penis or strap-on.

UNLOCK THE SECRET WISDOM:

Try it with a vibrating cock ring. The ring traps blood in the penis, keeping it harder, and will provide rumbly vibes to both partners. If a strap-on is involved, hardness is not a factor, but the vibes still feel good.

HARNESS THE FORBIDDEN POWER

Try a Dom/sub scenario with the person on the bottom calling the shots. They can issue commands like "Faster," "Nice and slow, there," "Suck my toes," or whatever they want their obedient sub to do.

THE PROPHESIED UNION
TWO HEARTS BEAT AS ONE

THE ORACLE'S INSTRUCTIONS:

The receiver lies on their back with their legs straight up into the air. The giver gets on their hands and knees and leans over their partner's body. The two partners press the palms of their hands together and look into each other's eyes.

THE RAVISHING:

Since you're already pressing your hands together and gazing into each other's eyes, go extra slow on this one to boost the romance and general swooniness.

UNLOCK THE SECRET WISDOM:

If you have the desire and the skills to take penetration deeper, the receiver can put their legs up over their partner's shoulder and explore the depths. (Be careful.)

HARNESS THE FORBIDDEN POWER

The Kama Sutra is big on teaching how to best please a vulva. Behold these ancient sacred skills: Warm up a vulva by playing with the hood of the clit. Gently push and pull it, twist it between your wet fingers, or tap it. Slowly unveil the clit, then tease it by flicking, tapping, or holding it between two fingers. Work up to a firmer rub. Then try going in circles or rubbing your hand back and forth across the clit or over the whole vulva.

29

THE MEETING OF THE ROYAL COURT

HOW DEEP IS YOUR LOVE?

THE ORACLE'S INSTRUCTIONS:

The receiver lies on their back, holding their legs in the air with their feet on each side of their partner's head. The giver gets on their hands and knees and leans over their partner's body to enter.

THE RAVISHING:

This has extremely deep penetration, so take it slow. Whether you are using a front hole or going around back, make sure the receiver is the one guiding how fast, hard, and deep it's going.

UNLOCK THE SECRET WISDOM:

Want to go even deeper? If the receiver has the flexibility, they can put their legs up over their partner's shoulders and (carefully) explore those depths.

HARNESS THE FORBIDDEN POWER

Since this position takes penetration about as deep as it gets, it will go better if everyone is well aroused before anyone puts a body part in anyone else. (This is true of all penetrative sex.) For a vulva, try sliding a wet flat palm over the vulva, bringing it slowly upward then back down. Slide a curled finger inside the vagina and press it against the upper wall. For a penis, stroke the shaft with a wet hand, making a twisting motion as you go up and down, being sure to make a pass over the head on the down stroke.

THE CONQUEROR

SURRENDER NOW

THE ORACLE'S INSTRUCTIONS:

The receiver lies on their back with their feet on the bed, then pushes their hips into the air. They keep their knees bent and their shoulders and upper arms on the bed. The giver kneels between their legs to enter. The receiver can keep their feet on the bed or lift them up so they're resting on their partner's thighs.

THE RAVISHING:

Both of you can thrust and grind against each other. Plus, the giver has their hands free and can easily stroke their partner.

UNLOCK THE SECRET WISDOM:

If the receiver is limited in how far they can or want to lift their butt, they've got options. The giver can hold their hips up with their hands. The receiver can support themselves on their hands and arms by holding their butt. Or you can make use of some positioning pillows and let them handle the job.

HARNESS THE FORBIDDEN POWER

Make a game of it by challenging each other with your thrusts. Try something—shallow and quick, slow circles, deep and hard— and see if your partner can match it. Or take turns doing the moving while your partner stays still and enjoys the ride.

THE QUEEN'S SECRET
ROYALTY CAN BE OH SO NAUGHTY

THE ORACLE'S INSTRUCTIONS:

The receiver lies on their back with their knees tucked up to their chest. They hold their knees with their hands, keeping them close to the chest and spread slightly. The giver kneels between their partner's legs and leans over, putting their hands by their partner's shoulders. The receiver can put their feet at their partner's sides or on their belly.

THE RAVISHING:

The person doing the thrusting should go slowly because the receiver is wide open and somewhat vulnerable.

UNLOCK THE SECRET WISDOM:

The angling here makes this good for givers with smaller penises or strap-ons. This also makes it good for folks wanting to try pegging with a small, non-threatening strap-on.

HARNESS THE FORBIDDEN POWER

This position was developed by the wife of a Vedic king. She was known for inventing new and interesting ways to have sex. This was supposedly the king's favorite position. Channel the spirit of this ancient queen and figure out something you can do to make this position your favorite. Is it having sex in a cape and warrior gear? Telling each other a dirty fantasy about forbidden love with an infuriating half-person half beast? Anal plus a G-spot toy for double penetration? Up to you!

32

THE DRAGON RIDER

BRING THE ROMANTASY INTO YOUR PRIVATE LAIR

THE ORACLE'S INSTRUCTIONS:

The giver lies on their back with their knees bent. The receiver squats over their partner, putting their feet on either side of their hips. The giver wraps their feet around their partner's hips, or, if their body doesn't go that way, just keeps their legs splayed out in whatever way feels comfortable. Hold hands for support and/or bonding.

THE RAVISHING:

It's the receiver s choice. The receiver is in complete control of the motion, the speed, the depth— everything. Whatever they want, they get.

UNLOCK THE SECRET WISDOM:

The receiver can change up their strokes as they please. They can sway or circle their hips or move up and down to thrust. (Careful, though. Penis breakage is a real thing that can happen.)

HARNESS THE FORBIDDEN POWER

If you want to try some romantasy-themed role play, the Dragon Rider is a great place to start. Fighters from enemy realms forced into proximity? Beauty and the Beast, but with a dragon? It doesn't have to be anything moral or acceptable in real life. In fact, it might even be better if it's not. Go ahead and play with the forbidden.

77

33

TWIN FLAMES

BURN AS ONE

THE ORACLE'S INSTRUCTIONS:

The receiver sits straight on the bed, folding one leg under themselves so they're sitting on it and extending the other leg along the bed. The giver mirrors their partner, putting their folded leg over their extended leg and their extended leg under their folded leg. Wrap your arms around each other for balance, or put a hand on the bed.

THE RAVISHING:

This isn't great for hard and fast thrusting, so embrace the slow and shallow penetration. Rock and grind against each other, sliding a hand or two down to add some stroking if you'd like.

UNLOCK THE SECRET WISDOM:

Take advantage of the face-to-face positioning to look your partner in the eye and tell them exactly how amazing they feel.

HARNESS THE FORBIDDEN POWER

If this doesn't seem like it's going be enough orgasmic stimulation for one or both of you, switch to mutual masturbation. For a vulva, try inserting two or three fingers inside the vagina, using the thumb to rub across or around the clit. Alternate pressure and deep thrusting or vibrating your hand. For a penis, try the 7-and-1 stroke: Stroke upwards along the shaft for seven strokes, then a single downward stroke, and repeat.

THE MOONLIT RIDE

FOR BAREBACK RIDERS ONLY

THE ORACLE'S INSTRUCTIONS:

The giver sits upright on the edge of a sofa, chair, or bed. The receiver sits on their partner's lap facing away from them to ride. The receiver has their feet on the floor and hands on the chair arms or mattress for leverage.

THE RAVISHING:

Whether you're going anally or vaginally, this is receiver's choice. They can move however they desire. The receiver can add a hand with a reach around or they can focus on themselves.

UNLOCK THE SECRET WISDOM:

For a non-penetrative option, the giver lavishes their full attention on their lap-sitter. They can play with their partner's nipples and squeeze or spank their ass while stroking their penis or vulva. Add neck and ear kisses and some whispered filthiness or words of love. Trade places afterward.

HARNESS THE FORBIDDEN POWER

The Kama Sutra says that the loins and thighs should slap together, like the sound of an "elephant's ears." Want to do that? Go right ahead. Go hard with the animalistic aspect and slap your body parts together, make some noise, and release your inhibitions.

THE SORCERER'S SNARE

GET COMPLETELY WRAPPED UP IN EACH OTHER

THE ORACLE'S INSTRUCTIONS:

Both partners sit face-to-face. The giver sits with their legs bent and the bottoms of their feet pressed together. The receiver wraps their legs around the giver's neck—the giver can provide a little help here—then crosses their ankles and holds onto their toes.

THE RAVISHING:

A gentle rocking motion works here. The giver can rock the receiver back and forth, or the receiver can hold onto their partner's shoulder to use it for leverage.

UNLOCK THE SECRET WISDOM:

This position doesn't have a ton of friction or movement, so amp up the stimulation with the wizardry of a special lube. Try a warming or cooling version or a special arousal gel.

HARNESS THE FORBIDDEN POWER

Adjust, adjust, adjust. This is a hard position to get into and a hard one to maintain. You don't get any points for doing it "right," so do whatever you need to make it work for you. The giver doesn't HAVE to press their feet together—position them another way if it feels better. If the receiver's legs only want to go up to the giver's chest instead of their neck—congratulations!—you've discovered your own new position.

THE KNIGHTING CEREMONY

KNEEL AND RECEIVE HONORS

THE ORACLE'S INSTRUCTIONS:

The receiver perches on the edge of a bed or chair and raises one leg up as straight as possible, holding onto their ankle with their hands. The other foot is on the floor. The giver kneels or squats on the floor to enter. The giver provides the balance for both of you.

THE RAVISHING:

The giver presses their hips against the receiver, holding onto their butt to bring them in even closer.

UNLOCK THE SECRET WISDOM:

The giver can use sorcery to bewitch the receiver's raised leg, giving it the attention it deserves. Try kisses on the ankle, licks behind the knee, and nibbles up the inner thigh.

HARNESS THE FORBIDDEN POWER

Prioritize comfort on your journey. If the receiver doesn't want to make their leg go straight, they can bend it or wrap it around their partner's waist. Plop a pillow or two for the giver to kneel on to protect their knees. If a chair isn't the right height, try a bed instead. Or do a version with the receiver on the table and the giver standing. The lovers always triumph—you will figure it out.

37

THE FAERIE SWING

JUST THE TWO OF YOU, LOCKED IN AN EPIC EMBRACE AND ROCKING TOGETHER

THE ORACLE'S INSTRUCTIONS:

Both of you sit down and face each other. The giver has their legs out in front of them, knees bent. The receiver sits on the giver's lap facing their partner and wraps their legs around their partner's hips. Hold onto each other's wrists or hands and lean back. Take turns leaning back, pulling the other person forward, dreamily rocking back and forth like you're on a see-saw. The movement is gentle and smooth.

THE RAVISHING:

This position is about deep connection and trust, so it's not for hook-ups. It's best for using with someone you want to go deep with. Move slowly, watching each other as you rock against each other.

UNLOCK THE SECRET WISDOM:

Use the Faerie Swing as a non-penetrative position. You can scooch a little toward or away from each other to adjust it. Try it with each of you touching yourselves (either simultaneously or take turns) or reach out to each other for mutual stroking.

HARNESS THE FORBIDDEN POWER

Make it an ultra-bonding experience by agreeing not to talk during it. Just stare into each other's eyes and feel your bodies rocking together. (Moaning and sighing are completely allowed.)

38

THE FULL SWOON

PREPARE TO BE OVERCOME

THE ORACLE'S INSTRUCTIONS:

The giver sits at the edge of a bed or chair. The receiver sits on their partner's lap and straddles them, sliding onto their penis or strap-on. Holding hands, the receiver slowly leans back until they are hanging upside down. For balance, the receiver can hook their legs around their partner's waist or hips.

THE RAVISHING:

The giver thrusts gently, being careful not to jolt the receiver's neck.

UNLOCK THE SECRET WISDOM:

The giver needs to hold on firmly and confidently to help the receiver feel safe enough to lean back into the full swoon. No one should be dropping anyone, but . . . scattering a few pillows on the ground will help the receiver feel more confident about relaxing into the position.

HARNESS THE FORBIDDEN POWER

If a vulva is involved, this position will require some extra clit stimulation. Since no one's hands will be free—they're making sure the receiver doesn't fall to the floor—try a wearable panty vibe or a couples' vibrator that provides internal G-spot stimulation combined with an external part that fits against the clit.

39

THE NYMPH IN SPRING

FROLICKING ENCOURAGED

THE ORACLE'S INSTRUCTIONS:

The giver lies on their back, legs comfortably extended in front of them. The receiver straddles their partner with one leg on either side and feet tucked under their partner's butt.

THE RAVISHING:

The receiver rocks gently against their partner's body—most of the movement is going on internally. The receiver squeezes their Kegel muscles or tightens their anus around their partner's penis or strap-on. (Mini-Kegel's refresher:

To find your Kegel muscles, tighten your pelvic muscles like you're trying not to pee. Feel that? Well done, warrior—you have discovered your Kegel muscles!)

UNLOCK THE SECRET WISDOM:

Sync the squeezes to the rocking motions or try varying them, shifting between long squeezes and quick fluttering. The receiver can tighten things up even more by squeezing their thighs together.

HARNESS THE FORBIDDEN POWER

Both of you will have plenty of ways to use your hands on each other. The receiver can rub their partner's shoulder and arms, stroke their chest, or lean over and lick and kiss their nipples. The giver can reach up and stroke their partner's chest, squeeze their thighs, or stroke their penis or vulva.

40

THE CELESTIAL CRADLE
LOCK INTO YOUR SACRED CONNECTION

THE ORACLE'S INSTRUCTIONS:

Both partners sit face-to-face and lift their feet to play with each other's nipples. Then they take hold of each other's forearms or hands and scoot forward so that they're butt to butt. The receiver puts their knees together and puts their feet on their partner's chest. The giver puts their legs outside of their partner's and puts their feet on their partner's shoulders or chest. Hold hands and look into each other's eyes.

THE RAVISHING:

This isn't so much about rigorous thrusting but about the connection between you. It's good for penetration, and you can certainly try, but it might work better if you do more gazing and less banging.

UNLOCK THE SECRET WISDOM:

If it's not working, try a plan B. Have the giver sit cross-legged. The receiver sits on their partner's lap, and both press their chests together. Then put your heads together and touch lips.

HARNESS THE FORBIDDEN POWER

You can go hard on the spirituality and mirroring aspect of this with lots of eye gazing and visualizing energy flowing between you. OR you can use it as boob footsie foreplay, then slide over on top of your partner for something more hardcore.

41

MAGIC MIRROR
FOR WHEN YOU CAN'T TAKE YOUR EYES OFF EACH OTHER

THE ORACLE'S INSTRUCTIONS:

Both people sit face-to-face. The receiver raises one hand in the air and wraps the leg on the same side around their partner's waist. The giver mirrors their partner, hand on their partner's hand and leg around their partner's waist. Feel free to stop there because it gets more difficult. If you want to be hardcore Kama Sutra, then both people lift the other foot and press them together in front of them as well, moving their feet together like they're pedaling a bike.

THE RAVISHING:

For this one, do whatever you can and call it a win. The fun of this is in the trying. If you can actually do it, good on you. You'll probably have better luck if you skip the foot peddling part, but go ahead and give it a go.

UNLOCK THE SECRET WISDOM:

Instead of penetration, use this pose to gaze into each other's eyes and stroke each other.

HARNESS THE FORBIDDEN POWER

The Kama Sutra lists many kinds of kisses. This is a good pose to try some of them out. The "throbbing kiss" is when the lips touch and you pulse the bottom lip. The "touching kiss" is touching your partner's lips with your tongue like a snake then kissing. The "bent deep" is a locking kiss with your tongues penetrating fully and hands cupping around the back of each other's neck.

42

THE DRAGON'S WING WRAP

WRAP YOURSELVES AROUND EACH OTHER WITH TANTRIC SEX

THE ORACLE'S INSTRUCTIONS:

The giver sits with their legs loosely crossed or with legs bent in front of them. The receiver sits on their partner's lap and wraps their legs around their hips. The giver penetrates the receiver and you both rock back and forth.

THE RAVISHING:

This is an ancient Tantric position for connecting on an extremely deep level. The motion is a gentle rocking and grinding together. The Dragon's Wing Wrap is especially good for people with vulvas because it gives more orgasm-inducing clit stimulation.

UNLOCK THE SECRET WISDOM:

Try the Tantric technique of placing your hands on each other's hearts, looking into each other's eyes, and synching your breathing. You can touch your foreheads together and feel each other's breath or lean in close to share some deep passionate kisses. When you feel like you're experiencing something spiritual, you're doing it right.

HARNESS THE FORBIDDEN POWER

If you're looking for less transcendence, more orgasms, feel free to reach down to stroke each other or you can modernize the position with toys. Depending on what kind of throbbing loins you have, you can use some vibrating nipple clamps, a strong wand vibrator, vibrating butt plugs for two, a prostate toy, a penis ring, or whatever else you desire.

43

THE UNION OF THE CENTAURI
STANDING DOGGIE STYLE FOR WHEN YOU MUST HAVE EACH OTHER

THE ORACLE'S INSTRUCTIONS:

The receiver stands with their legs apart and their hands on their thighs for balance. The giver stands behind to enter with penis or strap-on.

THE RAVISHING:

This is an excellent quickie position, the kind of position to use when you don't even want to wait to take your clothes off. Just a quick tug of the pants and you can start pumping. For more support, the receiver can stand near a bed, counter, or table and hold the hell on.

UNLOCK THE SECRET WISDOM:

The receiver can arch their back to change up the angle or press their legs together for a tighter feel. The giver can hold their partner's hips to pull them even closer, knead their ass cheeks, or reach around and stroke their chest.

HARNESS THE FORBIDDEN POWER

This is great for at-home quickies, but it's even better for forbidden quickies in places where you *really* shouldn't be having sex. Duck into a closet, a car, or a secluded spot in the forest. If true love hits you when you're out, you can slip into a restroom, a guest room at a party, or the tiny bathroom on an airplane.

LUST AND LOGIC NEVER

SEEM TO GO HAND IN HAND

—REBECCA YARROS, *FOURTH WING*

44

THE PALACE CAT
MEOW

THE ORACLE'S INSTRUCTIONS:

The receiver lies on their stomach, resting their upper torso on their forearms. The giver straddles their partner, holding both of their ankles to the side in one hand. The giver squats or kneels to penetrate and holds their partner's chin with the other hand.

THE RAVISHING:

Take advantage of the slightly askew ankle with slow, deliberate thrusts.

UNLOCK THE SECRET WISDOM:

Add some foot play by having the giver move both of their hands to their receiver's feet to give their partner a foot rub while they thrust.

HARNESS THE FORBIDDEN POWER

According to the Kama Sutra, in this position the receiver is supposed to go all-in with the cat concept, rolling around, purring, writhing their hips and arching their back. If you are both down, try a little predator/prey play with the receiver trying to "escape" and the giver trying to capture and pin their prey down. Or see if the giver can pet and stroke this feral kitty to coax them into letting them inside. (Again, big consent all around is necessary with all sex things, but even more so when you're doing something you don't usually do.)

45

THE UNEXPECTED TRYST
THIS IS HAPPENING NOW

THE ORACLE'S INSTRUCTIONS:

The receiver stands with their legs apart, bending at the waist and putting their hands on the floor. The giver stands behind to penetrate via penis or strap-on. They can hold onto the receiver's chest, hips, or thighs.

THE RAVISHING:

This is a position for when you need it hard, you need it fast, and you need it now.

UNLOCK THE SECRET WISDOM:

Some people want to be pounded while touching their floor, some do not. If the receiver is in that second category leaning on the back of a couch, table, or bed makes this position way more comfortable and doable.

HARNESS THE FORBIDDEN POWER

Just like romantasy characters don't immediately do it in the first chapter, the Kama Sutra stresses the importance of foreplay to raise desire. For a person with a vulva, it says, "The man should rub the yoni of the woman with his hand and fingers (as the elephant rubs anything with his trunk) before engaging in congress, until it is softened, and after that is done, he should proceed to put his lingam into her."

THE GOLDEN HIND

GROWLING RECOMMENDED

THE ORACLE'S INSTRUCTIONS:

The receiver gets on their hands and knees ala doggie style position. The giver squats or kneels behind, angling themselves for hard and fast thrusting. This works as a vaginal or anal position.

THE RAVISHING:

This position was inspired by the mating of deer. It looks like doggie but has a faster, rougher thrusting. The receiver arches their back up and down to create even more movement. Use it as a finishing move when you need to have an orgasm, like, NOW.

UNLOCK THE SECRET WISDOM:

If the receiver wants more direct stimulation, the giver can do a reach around to service their partner's penis or vulva via hand or toy. A wearable vibrator can also do the job for people with vulvas.

HARNESS THE FORBIDDEN POWER

Go all-in with the deer rutting theme by making it extra-animalistic. Make lots of noise and groan, sigh, and moan filthy/loving things to let each other know how much you're into it. If you've got enthusiastic consent all around (hugely important!), add some playful biting, unnecessary roughness, or a little bit of predator and prey play.

THE WEREWOLF'S HOWL

THE ANCIENT ART OF DOGGIE STYLE

THE ORACLE'S INSTRUCTIONS:

The receiver kneels on their hands and feet with their legs spread slightly. The giver kneels behind, their legs in back of their partner's, and grips their waist during penetration.

THE RAVISHING:

Move as the moon dictates. Slow pumping, fast humping, a combo of both. Your choice.

UNLOCK THE SECRET WISDOM:

The Werewolf's Howl is super adjustable, and you can change the mood and/or angles with small adjustments. For a tighter feel, trade leg positions so that the receiver's legs are inside the giver's and pressed tightly against each other. The receiver can also arch their back up or down to change stimulation for both people. Or add an edge of BDSM by having the giver hold onto the receiver's hand to keep them in place or using a spreader bar between the receiver's legs.

HARNESS THE FORBIDDEN POWER

This is known for being kind of a hardcore position, but you can make it extremely intimate by slowing it way down. Taking it to slo-mo helps you both feel *every* inch of each thrust.

THE MIDNIGHT VISIT

THE VERY BEST WAKE-UP CALL

THE ORACLE'S INSTRUCTIONS:

The receiver lies on their stomach with their legs slightly apart and pelvis lifted. They can support themselves on their forearms or lie flat. The giver lies over their partner's back, with legs on the outside, supporting themselves with their hands.

THE RAVISHING:

Go real slow on this one. It's a great lazy position for morning wake-up sex, sleepy good night sex, or extended weekend sex when you won't be leaving your bed chambers.

UNLOCK THE SECRET WISDOM:

Go for maximum cuddliness by having the giver brace themselves up on their arms to kiss and nibble on their partner's cheeks, eyes, ears, and neck. Try gentle nips, licks, and sucks. The receiver can lift themselves on their forearms and expose their neck and shoulders to get even more.

HARNESS THE FORBIDDEN POWER

Put the focus on the receiver's pleasure by putting a pillow under their hips and propping a vibe on it—anything from a small bullet vibe to a big industrial-strength wand will work. The giver can whisper sweet or filthy things into the receiver's ear, tell them how amazing they feel, or concoct a full-on sexy story to tell them as they slowly pump into them.

49

THE BREACHED BEDCHAMBER

WHEN IT'S NOT A DREAM

THE ORACLE'S INSTRUCTIONS:

The receiver lies on their stomach, pressing their head, chest, and arms into the bed with their hips slightly lifted. The giver lies over their partner to enter from behind. The giver holds their weight on their hands and knees—their chest is touching the partner's back, not crushing it.

THE RAVISHING:

Whether it's anal or vaginal, this is a good one for large penises or strap-ons. The giver can alternate their up and down thrusts with some slow hip circles.

UNLOCK THE SECRET WISDOM:

The receiver can prop their hips up on a pillow or sex wedge and lie on their hands. If they have a vulva, they can rub two fingers along each side of their clit or hump their lubed-up fingers or the palm of their hand. If they have a penis, they can rub the bottom of their shaft with a lubey hand or fill their hand with lube and make a tunnel to wrap around their penis.

HARNESS THE FORBIDDEN POWER

This is a great segue from a long, sexy massage. The giver can finish the massage by taking it a little more X-rated, bit by bit, rubbing their hands up their partner's inner thigh, and teasing them by brushing against their vulva or penis. When the receiver starts arching their back for more, make them wait a little longer, then go on in.

THE SIREN'S DANCE

SUCCUMB TO THEIR CHARMS

THE ORACLE'S INSTRUCTIONS:

The giver lies on their back with the receiver crouching over them and facing away. The receiver holds themselves on their hands and knees and slides their partner's penis or strap-on inside them. The receiver's hands rest on either side of their partner's legs, while their legs are wrapped against their partner's thighs for support.

THE RAVISHING:

This is a great position for the person on top to control the movement. They can roll their hips, rock back and forth, grind, or move up and down to thrust. It's also good for receivers who like to show off their ass and/or givers who like to look at that ass.

UNLOCK THE SECRET WISDOM:

Holding onto each other's feet and stroking them as you move together feels surprisingly grounding and connecting. Try lacing your fingers between each other's toes.

HARNESS THE FORBIDDEN POWER

Make good use of that butt. The receiver can tease their partner by rolling and gyrating their hips. The giver can squeeze, pull, knead, pinch, slap, or spank those cheeks. If the receiver is into it, the giver can use a paddle or whip across their backside or slide fingers or a sex toy inside.

THE SWORD IN THE STONE

DON'T PULL IT OUT

THE ORACLE'S INSTRUCTIONS:

The giver kneels on the bed.
The receiver squats back onto the
giver's lap, then bends over so
that their chest is pushed against
their thighs.

THE RAVISHING:

The receiver uses their hands to
press themselves back onto their
partner. The giver can help by
holding onto their partner's hips
or thighs to help move them.

UNLOCK THE SECRET WISDOM:

This takes some balance (and iron-
strong thigh muscles). For support,
the receiver can press their hands
to the bed or hold onto a sturdy
headboard. You can also try it on
the bottom steps of a staircase, with
the giver kneeling a few steps lower
than the receiver.

HARNESS THE FORBIDDEN POWER

Foreplay makes everything better. No one magically knows what
their partner likes, so you two get to learn each other. You can
start by touching your partner and getting feedback as you go
along. You can use actual words like "over to the side a bit more,"
or "faster," or just convey what's working via moans. You can also
masturbate in front of each other to see how your partner touches
themselves. Or you can put your hand on top of your partner's
hand on your penis or vulva and guide them.

THE ANGEL'S EMBRACE

SPOONING = SEX + HUGGING

THE ORACLE'S INSTRUCTIONS:

The receiver lies on their side. The giver lies behind them, wrapping their arms around their partner.

THE RAVISHING:

This is a spooning position, so move slowly to love each other up.

UNLOCK THE SECRET WISDOM:

Give the receiver more stimulation in front with a reach around. The giver can hold or play with their partner's penis or vulva, matching their hand motions to the thrusts. If the little spoon has a larger-sized body, try a long-handled vibrator like a wand for easier access.

HARNESS THE FORBIDDEN POWER

Try the Angel's Embrace for sleepy all-night sex. At bedtime, get each other close to orgasm, but don't let each other come yet. Go to sleep in each other's arms, mid-penetration or with the big spoon's hand cupping little spoon's groin. Boners will go soft, you'll shift positions and such, but whenever one of you wakes up, share some sleepy kisses, a few lazy thrusts, some loving strokes to each other's penis or vulva, or just press against your partner. Spend the whole night in sleepy, lusty bliss. When you wake up, you will be beyond ready for each other.

THE LIGHTNING BOLT

EXPERIENCE THE FURY OF THE GODS

THE ORACLE'S INSTRUCTIONS:

The giver stands with their legs spread and feet firmly on the ground. The receiver gets on their hands and knees in front of the giver, facing away. The giver lifts one of the receiver's ankles and puts it on their shoulder. The receiver holds themselves up on their hands like they're doing a handstand.

THE RAVISHING:

The giver can pump away as passionately as they can without knocking their partner down.

UNLOCK THE SECRET WISDOM:

You two might not be able to do this *exactly* as it's illustrated. Totally fine! The receiver can try spreading their legs wider and bending them slightly, or just use a chair, cushions, or even the side of the bed to prop themselves up.

HARNESS THE FORBIDDEN POWER

With no eye contact and not much skin-to-skin touching, this position doesn't seem like it would be intimate, but the intimacy comes through in other ways. Since you can't see each other, you need to work together to communicate what you want. Let each other know what you need via touch and sound.

THE CHARIOT
A RACE FOR TWO

THE ORACLE'S INSTRUCTIONS:

The receiver lies on the bed face down. The giver stands at the edge of the bed or kneels on the bed. They lift the receiver's legs with their hands to hold them up, ala the kid's wheelbarrow game.

THE RAVISHING:

This position allows the giver to use lots of different types of thrusting—quick and shallow, deep and fast, or pressing close and grinding. To switch it up even more, the giver can raise or lower the receiver's legs or open and close them like a pair of hedge clippers.

UNLOCK THE SECRET WISDOM:

This isn't inherently comfortable, so figure out ways to make it work. The receiver can try it on their hands or resting on their forearms. If that's not working, try a stack of firm pillows or some sofa cushions. If the giver doesn't have super strength, the receiver can carry more of their own weight on their arms and pillows. You'll figure it out.

HARNESS THE FORBIDDEN POWER

This wheelbarrow can travel. Turn it into a game by trying it in every room of the house. It can work on a bed, couch, table, desk, counter, or set of stairs.

THE BOUND SOULS

ALL TIED UP WITH PASSION

THE ORACLE'S INSTRUCTIONS:

The receiver lies on their belly and bends their legs, getting their feet as close as possible to their butt and holds their ankles. The giver kneels between their partner's legs, lifting their partner's legs off the bed and pulling them close to enter via penis or strap-on.

THE RAVISHING:

The giver can use forceful, deep thrusts. Use pillows under the receiver to tilt their pelvis and make it easier. And as always, if body parts aren't cooperating, abandon this treacherous path and find a way that works for you both.

UNLOCK THE SECRET WISDOM:

Experimenting with sensation play keeps the receiver in a state of high arousal and anticipation. Run things like a leather belt, a feather, or a silky scarf over the receiver's butt cheeks, back, and legs. The giver can also play with heat and cold by running an ice cube down their partner's thigh coupled with a dollop of warming lube dripping down their ass crack.

HARNESS THE FORBIDDEN POWER

If you'd like to try some bondage, the receiver is in a good position for a traditional hogtie. Use rope, bondage tape, or even just an old necktie to fasten the receiver's ankles and wrist together. You can lean even further into the BDSM aspects with ass play and spanking, and Dominance and submission.

THE DAGGER TO THE HEART

LOVE IS A DANGEROUS GAME

THE ORACLE'S INSTRUCTIONS:

The giver stands against a wall. The receiver stands and faces their partner, putting one foot against their heart. The giver holds their partner close to give them support.

THE RAVISHING:

Go with deep, solid thrusts.

UNLOCK THE SECRET WISDOM:

The position puts you in a combative stance. Go ahead and play with that. Try a little braggy trash talk. Don't be mean, unless you're into that, but tell each other what you're going to do with them or how hard you're going make them lose it.

HARNESS THE FORBIDDEN POWER

Ready to go into full battle mode? The Kama Sutra recommends scratching "when love becomes intense." The text recommends eight different types of scratches to be used when you are full of passion. You can lightly scratch your partner's neck, thighs, chest or arms, run your fingernails down each other's back, or dig those nails in when orgasm is nigh. Try the "half moon," where "the curved mark with the nails, which is impressed on the neck and the breasts" or "the jump of a hare," which is "when five marks with the nails are made close to one another near the nipple of the breast."

THE VAMPIRE'S CHOSEN MATE

TAKE A BITE OF EACH OTHER

THE ORACLE'S INSTRUCTIONS:

The receiver stands with their back against a wall with their legs spread. The giver stands to enter, holding their partner's hands against the wall.

THE RAVISHING:

The receiver circles their hips to provide the movement, or the giver can thrust away.

UNLOCK THE SECRET WISDOM:

This is all about the drama, less about taking a straight path to orgasm. If the receiver fantasizes about being ravished or taken, the giver can play into it by pinning their partner's hands against the wall and aggressively kissing them while they penetrate.

HARNESS THE FORBIDDEN POWER

Go even harder with the theatrics by adding biting. (With all the consent, of course.) The Kama Sutra describes several types of bites. If you both are down for it, try "discrete" (biting of the lower lip), "coral jewel" (marks left when the same spot is squeezed several times between the top teeth and lower lip), or "scattered clouds" (circle of irregular, small tooth marks beneath the breasts). If you like the idea of biting without the actual biting, try some toothless neck nibbling for some in-home vampire fan fic. "All the places that can be kissed, are also the places that can be bitten, except the upper lip, the interior of the mouth, and the eyes," reads the Kama Sutra.

SNARING THE ALPHA

HOLD ON TO WHAT YOU'VE GOT

THE ORACLE'S INSTRUCTIONS:

The giver stands, feet hip distance apart, and braces themselves with their legs. They can either lift the receiver onto their penis or strap-on or the receiver can jump up into their arms. The receiver wraps their legs around the giver's waist to stay put.

UNLOCK THE SECRET WISDOM:

Try this when you're taking the action from the couch to the bedroom and don't want to be apart for even a second. It's part sexy/part just fun.

THE RAVISHING:

The receiver holds on to rock against the giver.

HARNESS THE FORBIDDEN POWER

The giver can blindfold the receiver and carry them to a room that they've set up beforehand. Go ahead and set a theme for the evening. Go full dungeon master with an array of gear laid out on the bed like hand cuffs, floggers, and fetish clothing. Or prepare a romantasy playroom with some champagne (or mead) waiting at the bedside with soft music, scented candles, and this book open to a particular page.

THE HUNTER'S CAPTURE

YOU'RE COMING WITH ME

THE ORACLE'S INSTRUCTIONS:

Both people stand facing each other. The giver braces themselves with their legs and lifts the receiver, holding them up by their butt. The giver uses the crook of their elbow to hold their partner by the knees, and the receiver wraps their arms around their partner's neck.

THE RAVISHING:

This allows the giver to completely control the movement by moving the receiver's butt up and down over their penis or strap-on.

UNLOCK THE SECRET WISDOM:

Have the giver stand with their back against the wall for more support. But if you can't keep it going, take it to a couch or bed.

HARNESS THE FORBIDDEN POWER

This is great for G-spot and P-spot stimulation, but if you want more intense stimulation, take the pose to your bed so the giver can use their hands. For both G- and P-spots, the technique is similar. The giver slides a lubed finger inside their partner's vagina or butt, and presses, rubs, or taps on the upper wall, about an inch or two inside. Some people with vulvas can squirt with intense G-spot and clitoral stimulation, so throw down some towels first.

THE RISING PHOENIX

BURST INTO FLAME

THE ORACLE'S INSTRUCTIONS:

The giver stands against a wall. The receiver hops up on to their partner's body, clamping their thighs around the giver's hips and clinging to their neck. The giver holds onto each of their partner's feet with their hands.

THE RAVISHING:

The receiver controls the motion in this one by pushing themselves up and down on their partner's penis or strap-on while looking into their eyes.

UNLOCK THE SECRET WISDOM:

If you like the feel of this but can't maintain the position, have the giver sit their butt on the edge of a counter, table, or sturdy barstool.

HARNESS THE FORBIDDEN POWER

The Kama Sutra has an extensive section on hitting, including types of blows, where to hit, and the sounds to make when being struck. If you want to explore this a bit, you'll need to set some ground rules first. Choose a safe word, decide what will happen, and communicate throughout. You can go fancy and invest in a paddle or flogger. Or if you want to DIY it, you can use a ruler, hairbrush, ping pong paddle, or just an open hand.

BENEATH THE WATERFALL

GET DRENCHED WITH DESIRE

THE ORACLE'S INSTRUCTIONS:

The giver stands with feet hip distance apart and braces themselves with their legs. The receiver stands facing their partner and lifts a leg for easier penetration. Both people wrap their arms around each other for balance. If there's a big height difference, you can bend your knees to get parts lined up or the shorter person can stand on a sturdy step stool.

THE RAVISHING:

Move against each other however you can. Make sure you're hanging on.

UNLOCK THE SECRET WISDOM:

This is the rare position that actually works in the shower, but you need to be *extremely* safe. Create a fall-free area by putting down a non-skid floor mat and making sure there are sturdy things to hold onto like grab bars. And don't forget to use a silicone lube that will last under water.

HARNESS THE FORBIDDEN POWER

A detachable showerhead is a stellar way to make a vulva happy. Use it as an enhancement for penetrative sex or just on its own. Just get the water to comfortable temperature, point, and shoot.

CLIMBING THE TOWER

UP YOU GO

THE ORACLE'S INSTRUCTIONS:

The giver stands next to a wall with their legs apart and knees bent. They cradle the receiver's butt in their arm and hold them against their penis or strap-on, leaning back for more leverage. The receiver wraps their arms around their partner's neck and legs around their waist, using their thighs to hold on.

THE RAVISHING:

The receiver presses their feet against the wall for stability and to control the motion.

UNLOCK THE SECRET WISDOM:

Sharing your fantasies can be incredibly hot. Try whispering a fantasy—maybe a favorite romantasy scene?—in your partner's ear while you're moving together. (If you are fantasizing about someone else, the Kama Sutra says that's A-okay. It's called the "congress of transferred love." Maybe don't share that particular fantasy, though.)

HARNESS THE FORBIDDEN POWER

Keep a standing position going longer by investing in a sex swing. They'll keep you in position but without the feats of strength. There are simple ones that hang from a door jamb or more intricate versions with a padded seat.

THE FAE'S SURRENDER

GIVE IN TO YOUR FEELINGS

THE ORACLE'S INSTRUCTIONS:

The giver stands with their back against a wall or door jamb and knees flexed for support. The receiver wraps their arms around their partner's neck and circles their legs around the giver's hips, keeping themselves steady by wrapping their feet behind their partner's knees.

THE RAVISHING:

You don't have to get too elaborate. This is mostly about the swooniness of one of you whisking the other away in the passion of the moment.

UNLOCK THE SECRET WISDOM:

This is hard to maintain, so use it as a transport position to passionately take your destined love to a more comfortable room. If you like the feel of the position, but the giver's arms are starting to shake, do it next to a counter so that the giver can hoist the receiver onto the edge of a countertop and keep it going.

HARNESS THE FORBIDDEN POWER

Harness the weightlessness of taking this position underwater. The lifting that is difficult-to-impossible on dry land suddenly becomes easy when you're in a pool or a secluded pond. To avoid getting arrested for indecent exposure (and being too epically sexy), you'll need a private spot where you won't be interrupted. And make sure you use silicone lube to keep everything slippery because water is an anti-lube that, weirdly, makes everything drier.

THE CHIMERA

WILDLY IMAGINATIVE

THE ORACLE'S INSTRUCTIONS:

The giver stands behind their partner. They lift one of the receiver's knees into the air, holding them by the knee. The giver supports their partner with the other hand, either holding onto their thigh, their waist, or around their chest. The receiver has their leg as straight as possible behind them.

THE RAVISHING:

The giver has wide leeway for big thrusting.

UNLOCK THE SECRET WISDOM:

It can be super hot to watch yourselves in a mirror. And this is especially good for it because you are looking so very sexy. Angle yourself so you highlight whatever turns you on, whether it's watching your faces, a bouncing pair of boobs, a rear view, or....?

HARNESS THE FORBIDDEN POWER

Is using toys consistent with the Kama Sutra? Yes! It didn't exactly mention 10-speed wand vibrators, but it does talk about using dildos to enhance the experience. In honor of those early sex toys, try adding a dildo. Use a dildo on a penis-having partner for a different anal experience, or if the receiver has a vulva, add a dildo for double penetration.

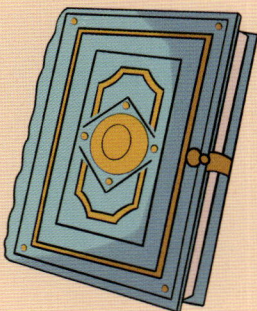